Personal Development and Work Experience Guide

Personal, Learning and Thinking Skills for the 21st Century

Edited by
John Mainstone and Ken Reynolds

opening doors
of opportunity

Personal Development and Work Experience Guide

This 5th edition published in 2011 by Cambridge Occupational Analysts Ltd
Sparham, Norwich, NR9 5PR

Editorial and Publishing Team

By John Mainstone and Ken Reynolds
Design and typesetting Simon Foster and Paul Rankin
Illustrations Diana Mainstone

© Cambridge Occupational Analysts Ltd 2011

British Library Cataloguing in Publication Data
A catalogue record for this book is available from the British Library.

ISBN 978-1-906711-12-2

Typeset by Cambridge Occupational Analysts Ltd, Sparham, Norwich NR9 5PR
Printed and bound in Great Britain by Clays Ltd, Bungay, Suffolk NR35 1ED

Disclaimer
*While every effort has been made to ensure that all information in this book is up-to-date
and accurate, and that all organisations listed are bona fide providers of opportunities for
young people to develop their personal, learning and thinking skills, inclusion should not
necessarily be assumed to be a recommendation. The authors do not accept any liability
for errors, omissions or apparently misleading statements, nor for any loss, illness, injury or
inconvenience resulting from the use of the information supplied. Readers must research
all options with extreme thoroughness and reach their own judgment regarding the most
suitable.*

Contents

Introduction

This book is about how you can develop your abilities in ways that will help you succeed in your future career. It is aimed primarily at young people aged around 16 to 18. We envisage that most readers will be working towards AS/A levels, Highers or equivalent and will be in Year 12 or Scottish Year 5 (Y12/S5) at school or college. You may be starting to research possible courses of higher education, perhaps contemplating a Gap Year before going to university, and wondering what on earth you'll be able to write in your application that will have admissions tutors queuing up to recruit such an admirable student!

Our goal is to present you with a series of suggestions and exercises that will give you an idea of the many opportunities available and an understanding of how best to match these opportunities to your own needs.

Should you wish to improve your grades by re-taking examinations or by seeking extra tuition for your current studies, we list colleges offering this type of provision. We also give details of Taster courses, provided by many universities and colleges to allow you to experience something of the academic and social life of an undergraduate student before you make a formal application.

Key Skills

Whatever you decide to do, try to look beyond the admittedly important elements of fun and excitement to think about whether your chosen activities will help develop the key skills needed for success in education, training, work and life in general.

The six key skills are:

- Application of number
- Communication - Written and Oral
- Improving your own learning and performance
- Information and communication technology
- Problem solving
- Teamwork/Working with others

These skills are relevant for everyone, from the youngest pupils in school to the most senior executives in large organisations. With the help of this book, not to mention time spent analysing your needs and exploring appropriate options, you should be able to improve the quality of your learning and performance by acquiring the ability to apply key skills in different contexts.

You should already have some knowledge of key skills, perhaps linked with a work experience programme in your school or college, together with curriculum enrichment activities. Key skills are also developed in the workplace and as part of university degree programmes. Not least, the achievement of key skills is recognised in the UCAS tariff for admission to higher education courses.

Try to identify skills you don't feel that you currently possess, or would like to reinforce, then think about how you could become involved in activities to help you develop those skills.

If you can provide examples from your own experience to illustrate the key skills, you will find that you have much of the material needed to complete the Personal Statement section of your university application. For more information on this, see our companion volume *60 Successful Personal Statements for University Application* edited by Guy and Gavin Nobes.

By tackling some of the projects outlined in this book, you could learn to lead with respect, to plan with safety and to participate with enthusiasm.

Once you feel motivated to develop your personal, learning and thinking skills, spend some time exploring the websites of the organisations listed on the following pages. The sheer number of agencies can be bewildering, so we have grouped them under headings to help you become aware of the range of opportunities available and decide what sort of activity best meets your needs. Please note, however, that many organisations offer such a variety of opportunities that they could easily be placed under several headings.

You can spend your time in the UK or overseas; you may be paid or you may have to pay a considerable sum in order to participate; you may choose a course of study or you may go on an expedition. Or maybe you've simply been stuck in the classroom for too long and need to get out in the fresh air and discover the delights of the great outdoors. It could be environmental work, sports coaching or some physically demanding adventure. The choice is yours.

Organisations listed here may be broadly based or may specialise in one particular type of project. Some activities may be paid, some unpaid, while some are predominantly focused on academic study. Typical offerings might include Volunteering (Community Development, Construction, Conservation, Teaching), Internships (Media, Marketing, Health, Tourism, Sports Coaching), Tours (Cultural, Ecological, Humanitarian) and Jobs (all over the world). We have also listed under this heading some associations - such as the Year Out Group - acting as an umbrella group for several separate providers.

Adventure Jobs   16+

If you are looking for a job in adventure activity, travel, water sports or skiing, you may find something suitable here. The site lists vacancies for activity instructors, group leaders, centre managers, resort staff, chefs, nannies, receptionists, drivers and support staff, among many others.

www.adventurejobs.co.uk

Africa and Asia Venture   18-25

AV, as it is generally known, recruits 18-25 year olds, who want to combine four to five months of travel, safaris, adventure, friendship and fun in a year out with teaching or coaching sports in rural primary or secondary schools, working with local communities or conservation work in the bush and on the Indian Ocean. You would normally start with a four-day in-country training course, then spend three to four months at your project, followed by one month of travel and safari. The latter could include seeing wildlife in African National Parks, visiting temples and palaces in India and Nepal, or adventure in Mexico. In Thailand, you would teach among the hill tribes for two months, followed by one month's project work, three weeks of travel/adventure opportunities and a five-day open water diving course.

www.aventure.co.uk

African Conservation Experience   17+

African Conservation Experience claims to be the most experienced organisation for conservation placements in Southern Africa. It can offer you the chance to work on game and nature reserves alongside conservationists, zoologists, wildlife vets and reserve managers. The organisation welcomes volunteers from all backgrounds, with no previous experience necessary, from the age of 17 upwards. Volunteer Placements are from one to three months, and you can combine two or more projects in one trip. You could join a placement as part of a Gap Year, in a summer break from school or university, or as part of a career break or sabbatical.

www.conservationafrica.net

Au Pair in America   18+

Working as an au pair in America can be a good way to discover the USA, as you can experience everyday life with a carefully selected American family and earn weekly pocket money by providing childcare as a nanny or babysitter. Whether you're looking for a year out or just want to work legally abroad, the exchange programmes on the Au Pair in America website give you free time to explore, study, travel and make new friends, together with professional support throughout your stay.

www.aupairinamerica.com

Blue Ventures

A not-for-profit organisation dedicated to facilitating projects and expeditions that enhance global marine conservation and research, Blue Ventures coordinates expeditions consisting of scientists and volunteers, working hand-in-hand with local biologists, governmental departments and communities, to carry out research, environmental awareness and conservation programmes at threatened marine habitats around the world.

www.blueventures.org

British Trust for Conservation Volunteers   All ages

BTCV has a successful history of environmental conservation volunteering throughout the UK and around the world. BTCV holidays take place all year round in some of the world's finest landscapes. Living, laughing and cooking together, you'll be busy all over, all the time. BTCV holidays don't just improve the environment - they're good for your health and could change your life.

www.btcv.org

BUNAC   18+

BUNAC offers a range of working holidays, including a summer camp counselling programme in the USA and Canada, flexible work and travel programmes to Canada, the USA, Australia, New Zealand and South Africa, and volunteering/teaching placements. These are open to 18 year olds and over in the UK, the USA and Ireland. Programmes last from five weeks to two years.

www.bunac.org

Camp America   18+

Each year over 7,500 young people take the opportunity to join Camp America and spend the summer in the USA, living and working either with children or 'behind the scenes' as support staff on an American Summer Camp. Following the end of your placement, you'll have up to two months to travel (in total your visa allows for up to four months placement followed by one month of travel but most placements end well within four months).

www.campamerica.co.uk

Changing Worlds   17+

With a wide variety of paid and voluntary placements worldwide, Changing Worlds offers destinations ranging from Australia, China and Ghana to Honduras, India, Kenya, Madagascar, New Zealand and Thailand.

www.changingworlds.co.uk

Cathedral Camps   16-25

Experience the hidden history of some of Britain's oldest and most beautiful buildings. Cathedrals, abbeys, minsters, chapels and parish churches make up a huge part of Britain's architectural heritage and every year teams of young people from all over the world move in to help refresh and conserve these buildings. Cathedral Camps have been running week-long residential breaks at cathedrals and churches throughout the UK for over 20 years - there are on average 20 camps at different venues, running each year throughout July and August. Cathedral Camps is now run by the UK volunteering agency CSV (Community Service Volunteers), mentioned below.

www.cathedralcamps.org.uk

Community Service Volunteers   16+

The UK's largest volunteering and training organisation, CSV provides hundreds of full-time volunteering opportunities across the UK that will equip you with life skills and enhance your CV or UCAS application. You will spend 4-12 months living away from home, supporting people in need and enabling them to develop or manage their own lives. As a CSV volunteer you will take on an important role that is valued by the community. You can use your skills and develop new ones, test yourself out in new situations, challenge your way of thinking, and make a genuine and positive impact on people's lives. CSV's placements are community-based, supporting a wide variety of people. You may be helping people with physical disabilities or learning difficulties, or supporting elderly people, children or young people.

www.csv.org.uk

Concordia   16-30

In addition to UK farm placements, Concordia offers an extensive international volunteer programme. Short-term projects bring together individuals from around the world to participate in two- to four-week projects in Western, Eastern and Central Europe, North America, North Africa, Japan and South Korea or Africa, Asia and Latin America. Medium-term projects usually last between one and six months, although they occasionally last for a whole year.

www.concordiavolunteers.org.uk

Coral Cay Conservation   16+

Coral Cay Conservation (CCC) is a not-for-profit organisation at the cutting edge of ecotourism. It sends teams of volunteers to survey some of the world's most endangered coral reefs and tropical forests. Its mission is to protect these crucial environments by working closely with the local communities who depend on them for food and livelihood. CCC currently has coral reef expeditions in Tobago and the Philippines and forest expeditions in the Philippines and Papua New Guinea. The organisation is largely financed by volunteers, who pay to participate in an expedition for anything from one week upwards. Volunteers require no scientific background and are trained on-site in marine or terrestrial ecology and survey techniques.

www.coralcay.org

Ecoteer

Ecoteer works by providing a site where volunteers can find work. By eliminating the middleman the cost of volunteering is greatly reduced giving more people the chance to volunteer abroad. All volunteering enquiries go straight to the projects so you can trust all the information you get is 100% accurate and up-to-date. Ecoteer offers cheap volunteer work and job opportunities at eco lodges, conservation, farm, teaching and humanitarian projects worldwide. It offers different types of placement such as ecotourism in Mozambique, a sea turtle conservation project in Costa Rica, humanitarian and teaching projects in Ecuador.

www.ecoteer.com

European Voluntary Service   18-25

The European Voluntary Service (EVS) is an Action of the Youth programme, implemented by the European Commission and YOUTH National Agencies. It allows young people to do a voluntary service in a local host organisation in a foreign country. Each year, about 4,000 volunteers participate in EVS. The annual funding is more than 300 million euro. The volunteer gains a variety of personal, professional and intercultural skills, and brings some added value and intercultural flavour to the host organisation and local community.

www.evsguide.eu

Experiment in International Living   16+

Your community service as an EIL Volunteer for International Partnership (VIP) could be working with a rural development project, volunteering in a health clinic, working with children or teaching English. VIP offers individuals or groups the opportunity to volunteer abroad in 14 countries: Argentina, Brazil, Chile, Ecuador, Ghana, Guatemala, India, Ireland, Morocco, Nepal, Nigeria, South Africa, Thailand and Turkey. Most programmes include language training and homestays with families - an excellent way to meet people and learn about local culture.

www.eiluk.org

Frontier Conservation   17+

The Society for Environmental Exploration (SEE), established as a non-profit conservation non-governmental organisation (NGO) dedicated to safeguarding biodiversity and ecosystem integrity, hosts a myriad of global conservation projects under the banner name of Frontier. With a long record of conserving biodiversity, discovering new species, building environmental awareness and developing sustainable livelihoods, Frontier offers 'hands-on' fieldwork, which benefits endangered tropical wildlife and their ecosystems and directly assists developing countries rich in biodiversity but poor in the capacity to manage natural resources.

www.frontier.ac.uk

GAP Enterprise

Providing independent advice through private consultation, GAP Enterprise uses its experience, knowledge and contacts to help you structure and plan a worthwhile gap year experience. Director John Vessey has led scores of expeditions to areas including jungle, arctic, desert, coastal water, mountain and high altitude environments. Former students have cycled across America, driven from London to Cape Town, reached Beijing overland, kayaked the Arctic Lofoten Islands, circumnavigated the world on horseback, traversed the Greenland ice cap, and reached the summit of Mount Everest.

www.gapenterprise.co.uk

Gapwork   17+

Whether it's skiing in the Rocky Mountains, volunteering in a South African safari park or tracking river dolphins in the Amazon that you want, you should find something suitable in the Gapwork activities section. Other sections include jobs, community development, sports and study abroad.

www.gapwork.com

Global Choices   17+

Based in London, Global Choices offers programmes classified in five types: Working Holidays, Internships, Teaching Abroad, Volunteering and Courses. Destination countries include Greece, Spain, Ireland, USA, Australia, China, India, Canada, Argentina, Costa Rica and Brazil, in addition to the United Kingdom.

www.globalchoices.co.uk

Global Vision International (GVI)   18+

GVI is a non-political, non-religious organisation, which through its alliance with over 150 project partners in over 30 countries provides opportunities for volunteers to fill a critical void in the fields of environmental research, conservation, education and community development. International partners include the South African National Parks Board, Diane Fossey Gorilla Fund, Jane Goodall Institute, Rainforest Concern and Kenyan Wildlife Service.

www.gvi.co.uk

Global Volunteer Network   18+

This network offers volunteer opportunities in community projects throughout the world, currently providing volunteer programmes through partner organisations in Alaska, Cambodia, China, Costa Rica, Ecuador, El Salvador, Ghana, Honduras, India, Kenya, Nepal, New Zealand, Philippines, Romania, Russia, Rwanda, South Africa, Tanzania, Thailand, Uganda, and Vietnam. The network continues to expand with new programmes continuously being researched and assessed.

www.globalvolunteernetwork.org

Global Volunteer Projects

Offers a variety of placements and projects across the world including medical placements, teaching projects, HIV awareness projects, journalism placements, conservation projects and orphanage placements. Their destinations include Ghana, Tanzania, China, India, Cambodia, Mexico and Romania. You could find yourself working at a Ghanaian TV station, at an orphanage in Cambodia or helping to preserve endangered Sea Turtles on the Pacific coast of Mexico. A month long trip to help out at an orphanage in Cambodia costs from £795 and includes food, accommodation and a language/culture course but not flights and insurance.

www.globalvolunteerprojects.org

Greenforce   17+

Much of Greenforce's current activity is focused on conserving coral reefs. Widely known as the rainforests of the sea, the reefs are home to a massive diversity of species and are much more than just a pretty underwater garden for divers to enjoy. On land, the competition for living space and resources is pushing wildlife into ever shrinking zones. The challenge for conservationists is to resist the pressure to deforest and exploit resources in favour of creating protected areas for wildlife and drawing up management plans for sustainable use. A huge part of the work that Greenforce does is also to contribute to improving the lives of fragile and sometimes threatened communities, such as the Maasai in parts of Kenya and Tanzania, and the Quichua Indians deep in the Amazon jungle.

www.greenforce.org

Habitat for Humanity   18+

An international charity working to end poverty housing around the world, Habitat for Humanity works in over 3,000 communities in 90 countries. You would normally spend around two weeks on location in a small community, actually building a house hand in hand with a partner family.

www.habitatforhumanity.org.uk

Help to Educate   18+

Help to Educate is a small registered charity that raises money to fund the education of child labourers in Nepal. It makes it possible to move children from dangerous working conditions and place them in a hostel where they can live and study. Most of the funds are raised by arranging for volunteers to teach in Nepal throughout the year. To teach in a Nepal school or help deprived children in a hostel can be a challenging, adventurous and worthwhile experience for people of any age and background.

www.help2educate.org

i to i   17+

In the past 12 months, i-to-i has: helped 5,000 people volunteer for projects in 23 countries; trained 15,000 people to Teach English as a Foreign Language (TEFL) and assisted them in finding jobs in Cambodia, China, France, Greece, Italy, Japan, Korea, Mexico, Nepal, Poland and Spain; and raised US$130,000 through its charity arm, the i-to-i Foundation, to buy much-needed materials for vital projects around the world.

www.i-to-i.com

International Voluntary Service (IVS GB)   18+

A peace organisation working for the sustainable development of local and global communities throughout the world, IVS GB is the British contact for Service Civil International, a worldwide network of like-minded voluntary organisations promoting peace and justice through voluntary work. By taking part in an International Voluntary Project, you will be working and living alongside other volunteers from all over the world and contributing to local community development. There are hundreds of projects to choose from, including environmental conservation on beaches in Morocco, help at a centre for children with disabilities in Latvia, work with elderly people in mountain villages in Japan, a community theatre in the Czech Republic, and youth work in Russia.

www.ivsgb.org

IST Plus   17+

With a IST Plus cultural exchange programme you can work, study, travel or teach in locations throughout the world. Work in the USA, teach in Thailand or China, travel around Australia and New Zealand, or study a language anywhere in the world.

www.istplus.com

Kibbutz Representatives   18-35

Living and working in a kibbutz community in Israel, carrying out the true principles of a socialistic society, having all work, property and profit equally shared by its members, can form the basis of an intriguing working holiday experience. A holiday with the possibility to meet, live and work with both Israeli youngsters and other kibbutz volunteers from countries and cultures far and near.

www.kibbutz.org.il/eng

Lattitude Global Volunteering   17-25

Lattitude organises voluntary work overseas in over 30 countries. Lattitude also organises similar exchange voluntary opportunities for overseas nationals in the UK. Lattitude volunteers work alongside staff in such roles as foreign language assistants, assisting with general activities in schools, caring for the disadvantaged, or in outdoor education and conservation work. Whatever the nature of your placement, it will always be a challenge. You could be working in an environment different from anything you've ever experienced, so you need to adapt to your responsibilities with maturity. As well as making a real difference to the lives of others, you'll certainly learn a lot about yourself.

www.lattitude.org.uk

Lean on Me

Aiming to improve the lives of people infected with or affected by HIV/AIDS, the Lean on Me organisers encourage volunteers to return to their countries as ambassadors for AIDS awareness and the hardships Africans face.

www.wecare4africa.com

Learn Overseas   17+

Specialists in India, Learn Overseas offer work experience placements, gap year programmes, career breaks, community-based projects and professionally led expeditions, mainly in and around Delhi.

www.learnoverseas.co.uk

National Trust

If you don't want to travel too far but are still looking for a way to make a difference in conserving the environment and the UK's heritage, the National Trust could have something to offer. As a volunteer, you can learn new skills and meet new people while working right at the heart of beautiful buildings, gardens and landscapes. The Trust also runs around 450 Working Holidays every year throughout England, Wales and Northern Ireland, where you could be involved with anything from carrying out a conservation survey to herding goats, painting a lighthouse or planting trees.

www.nationaltrust.org.uk/main/w-trust/w-volunteering.htm

Outreach International   17+

This specialist organisation has a wide variety of projects, all of them small, grassroots initiatives working with communities where volunteer work can make a big difference. There are one-month and three- to twelve-month projects in countries including Cambodia, Costa Rica, Ecuador, Galapagos Islands, Mexico, Nepal and Sri Lanka.

www.outreachinternational.co.uk

Oyster Gap Year   18+

Oyster offers projects working with children and teaching English in Brazil, Chilean Patagonia, Kenya, Nepal, Romania and Tanzania. Pre-departure training is included, as well as appropriate language training on arrival. The company also has some paid work opportunities in hotels and ski resorts in the Canadian Rockies and Quebec.

www.oysterworldwide.com

Personal Overseas Development (PoD)   17+

PoD provides the opportunity for you to volunteer and make a difference in parts of the world that are rich in culture, variety and natural beauty but where there is poverty or disadvantage. You may be on your gap year or wanting to volunteer as part of a working holiday abroad. Projects are currently available in Peru, Tanzania, Nepal and Thailand.

www.podvolunteer.org

PGL Travel   18+

PGL provides children's adventure holidays at its 33 activity centres across the UK, France and Spain. Every year it recruits over 2,500 staff to instruct, inspire and look after its guests, with vacancies for watersports instructors, adventure activity instructors, group leaders, language speakers, administrators, and maintenance, catering and domestic staff. There are also ad hoc ski rep positions for the peak weeks of the winter operating season.

www.pgl.co.uk/PGLWeb/recruitment

Prince's Trust Volunteers   14-30

The Prince's Trust helps young people overcome barriers and get their lives working. Through practical support including training, mentoring and financial assistance, the Trust helps 14-30 year olds realise their potential and transform their lives. The main target groups are those who have struggled at school, been in care, been in trouble with the law, or are long-term unemployed. As a volunteer with the Trust, you could have a powerful influence on the success of its programmes, and on the young people they help.

www.princes-trust.org.uk

Project Trust   17+

Based on the Isle of Coll, Project Trust specialises in year-long programmes rather than brief visits. You can choose from over 20 different countries, spending a year living, working and travelling outside Europe with a wide variety of work and a diverse range of cultures.

www.projecttrust.org.uk

Projects Abroad 17+

With a very wide range of projects, including teaching, care, conservation, medicine and journalism, Projects Abroad organises overseas voluntary work placements designed specifically for the communities where it works. The teaching projects focus on conversational English teaching and don't require TEFL qualifications. You could teach in Africa, Asia, Latin America or Eastern Europe, as part of a project in a school, university or orphanage. Teaching volunteers also often help with other activities, such as sport, music or drama for example. In journalism, you could work on a Chinese, Indian, Ghanaian, Mexican, Moldovan, Mongolian, Romanian or Sri Lankan newspaper or work at a radio station in Ghana, Senegal or Mexico or even a TV station in Mongolia.

www.projectsabroad.co.uk

REACH Adult

Not aimed primarily at school or college leavers, REACH seeks to match the skills of experienced people to the needs of voluntary organisations. REACH recruits and supports people with managerial, technical and professional expertise and places them in part-time, unpaid roles in voluntary organisations that need their help. Volunteers are placed with organisations near where they live, anywhere in the UK.

www.reachskills.org.uk

Real Gap Experience

Real Gap Experience is one of the leading independent Gap Year providers offering q comprehensive range of exciting volunteering, paid work, sports, adventure travel, language courses and career breaks in over 40 countries, from 2 weeks to 2 years. They can organise a complete gap year away unique to you (including flights and insurance) with a strong emphasis on security and safety. All their experienced advisers have taken their own gap years and will provide help and support to plan yours.

www.realgap.co.uk

Restless Development   18-28

If you are passionate about changing lives and want to make a difference to the community that you work with, you can volunteer to work for five to eleven months in India, Zambia, Uganda, Tanzania, South Africa or Nepal. You might find yourself helping vulnerable young people protect themselves against HIV, open a library or a youth centre, construct a smokeless stove or establish a recycling programme.

www.restlessdevelopment.org

Travellers Worldwide   17+

Offering a variety of voluntary projects lasting from two weeks to a year, Travellers Worldwide seeks to help children, adults, animals and entire communities in less advantaged countries. The only qualifications you need are a spirit of adventure and a sense of humour.

www.travellersworldwide.com

vinspired   16-25

Vinspired are young people who give up their free time to help their local communities. You might find them coaching a school football team, working at a community radio station or helping create a garden for local residents. Through the course of their voluntary work they gain valuable skills and experience that they can make use of in the workplace, such as team working, decision making and communication. Volunteers can learn practical skills too, such as designing websites or cooking. Having V on your CV is something that can make employers and universities sit up and take notice. If you are aged between 16 and 25, vinspired could be for you.

www.vinspired.com

Visit Oz   17-30

If you are considering a gap year in Australia before you go to university, after you have graduated or at any time before your 31st birthday, Visitoz guarantees to find you a job on the land or in rural hospitality, as well as providing agricultural or hospitality training. You must have a Working Holiday Visa (or other Visa allowing work) and be prepared to get your hands dirty. Outback farm or station work can include working with horses, cattle and sheep, tractor and header driving, bulldozer work, fencing, mechanical work, and chainsaw work; horse work may be at stables, in trail riding centres, on Host Farms, with racehorses, polo ponies, camp draft horses, or on cattle properties doing bore running, yard work, and maintenance; agricultural bike work is with cattle and sheep. There are so many jobs that it is possible to find something to suit the skills of everybody.

www.visitoz.org

Voluntary Service Overseas   18+

VSO has programmes and volunteers in 40 countries around the world. It offers a Youth Volunteering programme for young people aged 18 to 25, although its main volunteers are aged from 20 to 75 and must have a formal qualification and relevant work experience. Regular postings are for two years and volunteers are provided with accommodation and a local level allowance as well as air fares and insurance.

www.vso.org.uk

Volunteering England

Volunteering England works to support an increase in the quality, quantity, impact and accessibility of volunteering throughout England. You can volunteer for a very wide range of activities. From helping an elderly neighbour with their shopping to providing legal advice for a local charity, volunteers make a vital contribution to all aspects of community life.

www.volunteering.org.uk

Winant Clayton Volunteers   18+

Winant Clayton has over 50 years' experience placing volunteers in community projects in the United States. You could work with children, the elderly, the homeless, adults with mental health problems and many more. Previous experience is valuable but not essential. You will get direct experience of being part of a local community project in the United States. The work will be challenging and you will discover skills, potential and strengths that you never knew you had.

www.winantclaytonvolunteers.org

Worldwide Volunteering   16+

This organisation offers a 'search and match' database with over 2,400 volunteer organisations and 1.6 million placements throughout the UK and in 214 countries worldwide.

www.wwv.org.uk

Year Out Group   17+

Formed in 1998 to promote the concept and benefits of well-structured year out programmes, to promote models of good practice and to help young people and their advisers in selecting suitable and worthwhile projects, Year Out Group is a not-for-profit association of UK-registered organisations that specialise in this field. All the member organisations are carefully vetted on joining and provide annual confirmation that they continue to abide by the Group's Code of Practice and Operating Guidelines.

www.yearoutgroup.org

If you want to combine an adventure trek with an environmental, scientific or community project, you may find something suitable here. Expect to pay a substantial participation fee, for which you may have to raise sponsorship. Apart from being one of the best ways in which to fund your expedition, the experience of having to secure a considerable sum of money will help develop a range of skills before you even leave home! Expedition programmes give you the opportunity to develop many other important skills such as communication and time management. You'll be building confidence and self-esteem, in addition to learning to lead the expedition team and taking your turn to do so.

Australia Working Holiday   18-30

If you hold a valid UK passport and are aged between 18 and 30, you are eligible to apply for a Working Holiday Visa which will enable you to stay in Australia for up to 12 months, work with one employer for up to 6 months, study up to 4 months and leave and re-enter any number of times in the 12-month period. There is a huge variety of work on offer from bar work to fruit picking to working as a deck hand on a yacht.

www.australia.com/workingholiday

BSES Expeditions   16+

The British Schools Exploring Society organises extreme adventure and conservation expeditions in remote, wild environments. You could find yourself monitoring climate change in the Arctic, measuring biodiversity in the jungle or investigating human impact on the environment in mountainous regions. The aim is always to develop the confidence, teamwork, leadership and spirit of adventure and exploration of all expedition members.

www.bses.org.uk

Camps International   18-25

An award-winning expedition specialist that offers life-changing responsible travel experiences throughout Africa, Asia and Latin America. They offer gap year experiences in community and wildlife conservation in Kenya, Tanzania, Borneo, Cambodia and Ecuador. The programmes include four main elements; Community, Wildlife, Environment and Adventure, and the camps are located within communities and wildlife areas, away from the main tourist circuit, enabling all volunteers to become part of the local community and experience complete cultural immersion as a guest, not just a tourist. A two-month experience in Camp Kenya, which includes up to six weeks working in a school or other community project as well as snorkelling, safari and cultural trips, costs from £2,310.

www.campsinternational.com

Gap Guru   18+

GapGuru is a gap travel specialist offering a wide range of exciting gap year volunteering, teaching, travel and internship opportunities across Asia, Africa, South America and Europe. With GapGuru you could be caring for orphans in Africa, working on medical and journalism internships abroad, or even enjoying adventure travels in the Himalayas. It also gives advice on planning your gap year.

www.gapguru.com

Earthwatch Institute: 15-18

Earthwatch Teen Expeditions are designed specifically and exclusively for 15 to 18 year olds, and are completely different to any other experience teenagers can have. Working with projects all around the world, they're hands-on, engaging and meaningful, and provide unrivalled opportunities to undertake vital, peer-reviewed scientific field research under the supervision of skilled research teams in a professional setting. You can help show how much and how fast climate change is affecting the Arctic and what that means for the entire planet in Canada, or perhaps help to conserve Grévy's Zebra in the Samburu district of Kenya. The Earthwatch Institute offers a wide variety of experiences for all ages.

www.earthwatch.org

Gap Adventures

Gap Adventures arranges a range of adventure holidays around the world giving you the opportunity to step off the beaten track and experience authentic accommodation and local transportation to bring you face to face with the world's most fascinating cultures, customs and awe-inspiring wildlife. Adventures include a Cape and Dune experience in Namibia from £719 for a 13-day trip, or Roam Cambodia from £499 for a 10-day adventure.

www.gapadventures.com

Gap Year South Africa

Gap Year South Africa works extremely closely with under-resourced local South African communities. South African Gap Year projects contribute to social and economic development and address priority areas such as education, health, moral regeneration and social cohesion. Gap Year South Africa offers 3-week, 5-week, 3-month and 5-month project options in Cape Town, and volunteer projects include Teaching and Education, Sports Coaching, Performing Arts, HIV/AIDS Awareness, Care Work, Medical and Veterinary projects and Environmental Awareness, Scuba Diving, Marine Conservation and Surfing Projects. For example, working on a marine conservation project in Cape Town costs from £1,295.

http://gapyearsouthafrica.com

InterRail

Offers information on how to travel around Europe by train including planning your journey, timetables, maps and passes. The most popular product is the Global Pass which gives you flexible train travel in 30 countries.

www.interrailnet.com

Jubilee Sailing Trust   16+

The Jubilee Sailing Trust (JST) is a charity that aims to promote the integration of people of all physical abilities through the challenge and adventure of tall ship sailing. The JST owns and operates two tall ships - LORD NELSON and TENACIOUS - the only two vessels in the world that have been purpose-designed and built to enable a crew of mixed physical abilities to sail side by side on equal terms. If you take on the tall ship challenge with the JST, it could be a short hop around the British coast, a four-week transatlantic challenge, a week's island hopping in the Canary Islands or the Caribbean, or a place in the European Tall Ships' Race

www.jst.org.uk

Madventurer   17+

As a volunteer, you become part of the Mad Tribe. The spirit of volunteering brings together all shapes and sizes and accents. Each year there is a Mad World Ball in Newcastle upon Tyne, for reunions and reminiscing of the time you've weathered and treasured together. Madventurer rural projects focus on building basic infrastructure to assist local community development. The key focus is youth development and the provision and improvement of health, education and sanitation facilities such as schools, clinics, toilets, water storage tanks, community centres and sanitation facilities. Venturers also have the opportunity to teach English and other subjects in local primary schools, as well as getting involved in extracurricular activities such as sports, art and drama.

www.madventurer.com

Outward Bound Trust   11 to 17+

Outward Bound seek to help young people have access to safe, adventurous experiences - from abseiling to zip wiring - through which you can raise your self-esteem, realise your full potential and achieve more than you ever thought possible. Among the 'Ultimate adventures for individuals' are UK expeditions in the Scottish Highlands, the Isle of Skye and Wales, and global expeditions in Transylvania (Romania), Sabah (Malaysia), and South Africa.

www.outwardbound.org.uk

Overseas Job Centre

This site lists around 100 cheap (sometimes free) volunteer work opportunities around the world from tourism and catering to teaching or working with animals. It gives advice on planning your gap year as well as a useful list of websites for reference and further information.

www.overseasjobcentre.co.uk

Quest Overseas   17+

Specialists in Africa and South America, Quest offer 'Combined Gap Expeditions', in which you can learn a language, work on a community or conservation project and then explore the best of the surrounding countries. This could lead, for example, to Community Development work in Tanzania or a Game Reserve project in Swaziland, together with exploration of southern Africa, or an Animal Sanctuary project in Bolivia, together with exploration of the Andes.

www.questoverseas.com

Raleigh International   17+

The Raleigh overseas programme enables participants aged 17 to 24 from all over the world and from all backgrounds to undertake a blend of mental and physical challenges. The full 10-week programme consists of three distinct project phases - sustainable community and environmental projects plus an adventure phase. There are also five-week programmes, which combine your choice of either a community or environmental project with a team-based adventure challenge. Destinations include Costa Rica & Nicaragua, India and Malaysia (Borneo).

www.raleighinternational.org

Royal Geographical Society

Every year the Society supports between 40 and 50 teams of students and researchers to get into the field with a Geographical Fieldwork Grant, the Society's longest-running grant scheme. The three independent travel grants support challenging and inspiring geographical journeys and expeditions and are worth up to £3,000. Full details of the different grants available can be found on the website.

www.rgs.org

Tall Ships Youth Trust   16+

The Tall Ships Youth Trust owns two 60-metre square-rigged ships. They are operated by Tall Ships Ltd., one of the charity's subsidiaries, and work 12 months of the year both around the UK and abroad, offering Tall Ship Adventure Sailing Holidays.

www.tallships.org

The Leap   17+

The Leap offers adventurous team or solo voluntary work placements in Africa, South America, Asia and Australia. All placements combine conservation, eco-tourism and community projects, otherwise known as the Three Leaps. This mix of challenges and experiences, combined with adventure travel in the form of scuba diving, kite surfing, white water rafting, riding or polo, should serve to broaden your horizons and surpass your expectations.

www.theleap.co.uk

Tour Dust

Tourdust is a revolutionary adventure travel agent for independent travellers who are looking to book activity holidays, adventure holidays and tours from expert local operators all around the world. Experiences offered by Tourdust include Inca Trail treks, Galapagos Cruises and trekking in Morocco's Atlas Mountains alongside a host of other unique travel experiences such as Safaris in the Masai Mara and Sea Kayaking in the Aegean.

www.tourdust.com

Trekforce Worldwide   18+

With over 20 years' experience of organising expeditions - that combine real adventure with a serious purpose - in the rainforests, deserts and mountains of the world, Trekforce Worldwide run one-to five-month expeditions and gap year programmes that tackle tough conservation or development projects, and can be followed by intensive language courses and long-term teaching placements in rural communities. They also offer a series of two-to three-week Extreme Expeditions to the most testing environments around the world, designed to push you to the very limit.

www.trekforce.org.uk

VentureCo   17-20

VentureCo's multi-phase travel programmes incorporate development projects, expeditions and adventure travel in Asia, Africa, South America and Central America. The ventures are a combination of complementary phases. For example, in South America you would combine a Spanish language phase with a Project phase and an Expedition phase to make one venture. Each phase reveals a different aspect of your host country and together they produce one memorable travel experience.

Participation in the venture is the most important element of its success: venturers are team players with considerable input into the everyday running of each phase. Venturers are aged between 17 and 20 and applications are taken from the UK and overseas.

www.ventureco-worldwide.com

Wind, Sand and Stars - Sinai Summer Expedition   16-23

The Summer Expedition is a three-week journey through the Sinai with the local Bedouin. It combines trekking in the high mountain region, learning about team management and survival, with working on community-based projects for the Bedouin. The Expedition runs from mid-July to mid-August and is open to students aged between 16 and 23. During the expedition you will work on a local Garden Regeneration project alongside the local Bedouin tribes within a mountain area. The projects are chosen in conjunction with the Bedouin and designed to ensure that they meet a very real need.

www.windsandstars.co.uk

Woodlarks Campsite Trust, Surrey   16+

Situated in twelve acres of beautiful Surrey countryside, Woodlarks Campsite enables children and adults with disabilities to enjoy a host of activities they may never have thought possible.

Woodlarks camps can be as tranquil or as adventurous as you want them to be.

www.woodlarks.org.uk

World Challenge Expeditions   17-24

On a World Challenge overseas expedition, you could soon be trekking through the jungles of Borneo or climbing Mount Kenya. Many expeditions are organised for school groups but you can participate as an individual. There are one-month expeditions suitable for young people up to the age of 22, with destinations including the Andes and Amazon (Peru), Borneo, Central America (Belize, Mexico and Guatemala), East Africa (Kenya), and India and Himalaya.

www.world-challenge.co.uk

Worldwide Experience

Worldwide Experience allows you to work with animals while contributing to global conservation and community programmes. They specialise in conservation projects in South Africa but also offer animal rehabilitation projects, veterinary experiences and game ranger courses. Other activities can include sports coaching and teaching and marine conservation. All projects are run by specialists in their field who are specifically trained to impart their skills and experience. For example a two-week programme working on a conservation project in the Shamwari Game Reserve in South Africa, where you assist in the work of an award-winning conservation team, costs from £1249.

www.worldwideexperience.com

Work Experience

Learn how business works…and get paid for it in some cases! You may be carrying out research, designing prototypes, planning projects, handling customers' needs or devising new working methods. Projects vary depending on company needs.

BBC

The British Broadcasting Corporation has work experience placements available in just about every area of BBC activity across the UK. Whatever your age and whichever area you're interested in, there could be something right for you, from advertising, charitable work or entertaining to journalism, music or the World Service. All placements are unpaid and can last anything from a few days to four weeks. Competition is fierce, so before you apply you'll need to consider what you can offer and what you'd like to achieve. Are you good with computers? Have you worked in hospital radio or written articles for your local or college magazine? What do you hope to gain from the placement? What are your ambitions for the future? These are the kind of questions you should be asking yourself.

www.bbc.co.uk/jobs

Engineering Education Scheme (England) 16-17+

This programme links teams of four Year 12 students and your teacher with local companies to work on real scientific, engineering and technological problems.

www.thescheme.org.uk

Gap Medics 16-25

Gap Medics offers the opportunity for those embarking on a career in medicine/nursing to gain valuable and interesting medical work experience in a safe and supported environment. It has provided once-in-a-lifetime medical experiences for over 2,000 students around the world. The cost of the experience varies but includes Hospital work experience placement; Professional supervision & clinical teaching; Safe, sociable accommodation in our own houses; All your food; Airport welcome & transfer; Help with all your preparations; 24/7 support from our expert teams in the UK and overseas. For example, a two-week placement in India costs from £990.

www.gapmedics.com

GlaxoSmithKline

Summer placements typically last 10 to 12 weeks. We are interested in students who can add value to our company through their skills and experience and who, after graduation, may be able to fill some full-time roles (subject to success at selection events). As well as developing the technical skills of students, our summer placements will provide you with an insight into life and work in GSK. Placements may be available in marketing or purchasing sectors of the industry.

www.gsk.com/careers/uk-undergraduate-plac.htm

ITV 14+

ITV offers the 'ITV Experience'. Twice a year (usually in February and September), application to join the ITV Experience Pool is opened up. If successful, you may be offered a two- to four-week Experience in various ITV departments working with fully qualified teams. It gives the opportunity to experience the real world of media industry.

www.itvjobs.com/work-experience-and-apprenticeships

John Lewis Partnership   16-17+

John Lewis offer an opportunity to spend two weeks in a department store, where you can gain an insight into the world of retailing. Placements normally take place in selling departments but John Lewis also accommodate students in other areas of the business if you have a particular interest.

www.jlpjobs.com

Pinsent Masons - Gap Year (Pre-University)

International Law firm Pinsent Masons offer a pre-univeristy Gap Year Programme which runs from September to April and is available in their Birmingham and Leeds offices. It offers solid, first-hand experience of commercial law before you start university. If you're serious about a career in law, it's a chance to build a CV that will help you stand out from your peers. It will also give you the opportunity to earn some money to put towards travel or university costs.

http://graduate.pinsentmasons.com

Year in Industry   17+

The Year in Industry scheme offers paid, degree-relevant work placements in a year out before or during your university course. With opportunities in all branches of engineering, science, computing and business management, you can undertake real projects and learn how business works. The skills you develop should enhance your university education and maximise your graduate job prospects. Many companies view the scheme as an important part of their recruitment programme, and go on to sponsor placement students through university.

www.yini.org.uk

See Also

Science, Engineering and Medicine

Many of the opportunities listed here give you the chance to make things happen by taking scientific knowledge and converting it into working products, systems and processes.

ATOM (Advanced Topics on Medicine) Conference

This is a one-day conference designed to help Years 12 and 13 (Sixth Form) students who want to hone their UCAS applications for Oxford, Cambridge and all other UK medical schools. It includes the following areas - impartial advice on UK medical schools, mock medical school interviews with feedback, before and after interview techniques, optional DVD of personal interviews and optional UCAS personal statement review.

www.atomconference.com

British Association   14-19

The British Association for the Advancement of Science organises National Science Week in March with over 2,000 scientific, engineering and technology events occurring throughout the country and the Festival of Science in September which includes dialogue events for 14-19 year olds. Information is sent direct to schools.

www.britishscienceassociation.org

Embryo Veterinary School, Devon   17+

The Embryo team of experienced vets and academics offer a three-day course for aspiring vets, giving detailed analysis of Veterinary Science degree courses, and honest insight into the realities of the job. Set in rural Devon, the course provides an opportunity to spend time in a working veterinary practice environment.

www.embryovets.com

Engineering Education Scheme in England   16+

The scheme, sponsored by the Royal Academy of Engineering, aims to help young people achieve their full potential in engineering, science and technology. Students are given the opportunity to work in an engineering environment for a few months before taking A levels.

www.thescheme.org.uk

Headstart Courses   16+

A well-established education programme whose aim is to encourage students interested in mathematics or science to consider technology-based careers. It provides an opportunity for you in Year 12/S5 to spend up to a week at university prior to making your UCAS application.

You have to pay to attend, typically around £235. This includes all accommodation and meals during the course, but not travel costs to and from the university. Some bursaries are available where financial hardship would prevent attendance, and your school may help with the course fee.

www.headstartcourses.org.uk

INSIGHT Courses   16+

INSIGHT Courses are for the young woman with a genuine interest in becoming an engineer. Applicants spend a week at university living in student residences. You will have opportunities to find out about different fields of engineering, spend a day with an engineering company and meet other women who are working successfully in engineering and technology-based careers.

www.insightcourses.org.uk

Medlink

Medlink is a four-day course for young people considering a career in medicine. It gives delegates the opportunity to listen to and discuss medical school admission and careers in medicine with Deans from a number of medical schools, as well as advice on surviving medical school given by medical students, and gives the chance to talk with practising doctors and medical students. The course is valuable for students in years 12 and 13.

www.medlink-uk.org

Medsim

Medsim is a three-day residential course held at the Nottingham University School of Medicine. Medsim offers a rich selection of patient contact and practicals that will considerably strengthen the young person's UCAS application. Most importantly, the experience of working under supervision in small groups, with real patients and equipment, has the benefit of allowing young people to experience what it is like to be a doctor, to deal with patients, to be on-call and work under pressure.

www.medlink-uk.com/medsim/faq.htm

Pre-Med Course

Pre-Med Course is a one-day medical careers course run by a team of doctors. The course gives impartial careers information to anyone considering medicine as a career. Topics covered include application procedures, interviews, medical school curriculum, practical demonstrations etc.

www.premed.org.uk

Royal Institution   All ages

An important part of the work of the Royal Institution is to promote an understanding of science in young people. To further this aim, lectures and events are held throughout the year specifically targeted at the new generation of budding scientists. The lectures for young people are held during the Christmas holidays.

www.rigb.org

Salters' Chemistry Camps   14-16

Hugely popular four-day residential camps for fifty 15 year olds at universities throughout the UK, packed with exciting chemistry and social events. The aim of the camps is to encourage young people to participate in the fun of chemistry and motivate them to develop awareness of and a long-term interest in the subject.

www.salters.co.uk/camps

Smallpeice Trust   18+

The Trust offers four-day residential courses at universities, allowing you to develop your interest in engineering by exploring specific areas such as aerospace or supercomputing in engineering, placing you alongside real engineers, professionals and technical specialists.

www.smallpeicetrust.org.uk

Workshop Conferences   17+

The Workshop offers two- and three-day residential conferences, covering such career/degree-related topics as: nursing, medicine, physiotherapy, psychology, veterinary science and working with animals.

www.workshop-uk.com

Business Skills

From typing and temping to word processing or web design, courses listed in this section can both enhance your key skills and improve your future employment prospects. They can increase your effectiveness in higher education making it easier to update research reports and essays.

Oxford Media and Business School   17+

The School's 'Gap Year Life Skills' course is designed to give you an early taste of a university style environment, together with training in key Life Skills such as the use of the latest IT software. The Careers Direct placement bureau will then help you find temping work, which can be invaluable both for later university submissions and for earning cash to fund the rest of your Gap Year.

www.oxfordbusiness.co.uk

Pitman Training 17+

There are more than 90 Pitman Training Centres all over the UK, Ireland and the Middle East, training 50,000 people every year. Courses are available in areas such as IT and Business skills, including Bookkeeping and Accounts, Web Design, Shorthand, Spreadsheets and Word Processing.

www.pitman-training.com

Quest Business Training 16+

Quest Business Training was formed following the merger of Queen's, St. James's & Lucie Clayton. Quest welcomes school leavers, gap year students and graduates. Mature applicants are also encouraged to apply, while our popular summer programmes are open to pupils from Year 9 upwards. The strong teaching staff, challenging curriculum, variety of teaching methods, warm atmosphere and vocational approach to training all contribute to the confidence gained from succeeding here.

The six-week Business Skills Course is popular with gap year students and graduates who are in a hurry to gain skills and move into the workplace. There is also a one-term Intensive Course offering a choice between learning shorthand or extra IT skills with an external qualification. Other courses include the three-term Marketing and Business Skills course and the two-term Executive and Personal Assistant's course.

www.questcollege.co.uk

Workshop Conferences 17+

The Workshop offers two- and three-day residential conferences, covering such career/degree-related topics as: business and management, and criminal law.

www.workshop-uk.com

Sports Related

Whether you are new to a sport or already experienced, these courses can enhance your performance. Achieving instructor status could provide opportunities to teach a sport to fellow undergraduates and to represent your university in e.g. golf, tennis, sailing, rowing, football.

David Lloyd Leisure   15+

With 79 clubs across the UK, David Lloyd Leisure could help you improve your health and fitness. The group's racquets facilities include 500 tennis courts (over half of which are indoor), 100 badminton courts and 85 squash courts.

www.davidlloydleisure.co.uk

Exsportise   9-16

Coaching in tennis, field hockey, golf and football. Residential and day courses for all abilities. Activities occur during Christmas, Easter and the summer holidays. Locations: Seaford College, Sussex, Oundle School, nr Peterborough and Clayesmore School, Dorset.

www.exsportise.co.uk

Flying Fish 17+

This organisation offers professional training for yachtmasters and instructors in yachting, dinghy sailing, windsurfing, surfing, diving, snowboarding and skiing. As an experienced yacht skipper or instructor, you can then spend time earning money from your favourite sport.

www.flyingfishonline.com

International Academy 18+

Become a ski or snowboard instructor on a 5- to 12-week gap year or career break course. Experience world class resorts and gain recognised CSIA, CASI, NZSIA or SBINZ instructor qualifications. Resorts include Banff / Lake Louise, Whistler Blackcomb, Sun Peaks Resort and Castle Mountain in Canada. Summer courses are also available at Mt Hood in the USA and Cardrona Alpine Resort in New Zealand. Courses in scuba diving, sailing and surfing.

www.international-academy.com

Jonathan Markson Tennis 10+

A graduate of Christ Church College, Oxford, Jonathan Markson is a former captain and coach of the Oxford University 'blues' tennis team and an international player for Scotland. His company offers tennis holidays and tennis camps in England, Portugal, Spain, Italy, Cyprus, South Africa, Tunisia, Czech Republic, Hungary and the USA.

www.marksontennis.com

NONSTOP Adventure 17+

NONSTOP Adventure is a family-owned company that runs mountain biking, sailing, skiing and snowboarding training courses. Whether your passion is for the sea or the mountains, there is a course for you. In most cases courses will result in gaining internationally recognised instructor qualifications that could open up exciting employment opportunities worldwide. All courses are run by the industry's top professionals and focus on general improvement as well as gaining professional instructor qualifications. All abilities welcome. ATOL protected.

www.nonstopadventure.com

Peak Leaders   17+

Peak Leaders' Mountain Bike, Surf, Ski and Snowboard courses ensure you will be improving your technical skills, gaining snowsports qualifications, and increasing your understanding of mountain environments, safety and team leading. At the same time, you'll be experiencing life in another culture such as in Canada, New Zealand, South America, France or Switzerland. There are also nine-week summer break, southern hemisphere courses, with the emphasis on travel and adventure.

www.peakleaders.com

Sporting Opportunities

Sporting Opportunities offer sports coaching volunteer projects which give you the chance to travel to Africa, Asia and South America with likeminded people and volunteer in the community as a sports coach. You will coach sports to children from disadvantaged backgrounds, play sport in the local community and return home with some unforgettable memories. There are a variety of volunteer sports projects to choose from including football, hockey, rugby, netball and many more. You could find yourself coaching football in India, Argentina or Ghana, or perhaps netball and hockey in South Africa.

www.sportingopportunities.com

United Through Sport

United Through Sport is a UK-registered charity that supports sport and recreation projects in Developing World countries. It particularly focuses on four outreach programmes in South Africa, working with the Umzingisi Foundation, to deliver sporting opportunities for over 15,000 disadvantaged children. The sports programmes are run in local communities focusing on rugby, netball, cricket, soccer, hockey, swimming and tennis, and offer the opportunity to volunteer as a sports coach.

www.unitedthroughsport.org

See Also

Language Skills

Learn a new language or simply develop your existing linguistic ability! Effective communication is a vital ingredient in every sphere of human activity.

Cactus Language

Cactus Language help over 15,000 people every year learn more than 30 languages, in 60 countries and 500 destinations worldwide. They provide thousands of different courses around the world and can create or tailor any programme specifically to individual needs. Cactus also provide courses for children, under 18s, families and the over 50s. There is the opportunity to learn Spanish in Buenos Aires or Italian in Florence. They also offer TEFL courses for those who wish to teach English abroad.

www.cactuslanguage.com

CESA Languages Abroad   16+

A Languages for Life courses immerses you in a language, teaches you key language skills and provides you with the opportunities to put these skills into daily practice. You will gain a wider and richer knowledge of the vocabulary, grammar and syntax of the language or, at a higher ability level, you can add layers of understanding in the form of nuance and cultural reference critical to real language competence. Students of European languages can see tangible results over an 8- to 16-week period, although you can study for longer. If studying Arabic or Russian, you may need 8 to 20 weeks for serious linguistic improvement, and 12 to 24 weeks for Japanese or Chinese.

www.cesalanguages.com

OISE

OISE offers intensive language courses in English, French, German and Spanish with either intensive short courses or extended programmes for exam preparation. Students are taught in small groups of 4 or 8 maximum per class at all levels.

The language schools can be found in the UK, France, Germany, Spain, Canada, United States and Australia and are open all year round: during the academic year, during the summer and other vacations.

www.oise.com

Rotary Youth Exchange   16+

Each year the Rotary Youth Exchange programme sends literally thousands of young people, aged up to 25 years, on long- and short-term exchanges, special interest camps and tours. These aim to promote an insight into another country's way of life, traditions and culture, and develop to lasting friendships.

www.youthribi.org

See Also

Opportunities listed here include the chance to work with leading professionals, to develop your individual performing skills and to experience the buzz of live performance.

European Union Youth Orchestra   14-24

The Orchestra is made up of some 120 players, representing all 27 member countries of the European Union (EU). The players are selected each year from over 4,000 candidates aged up to 24, who take part in auditions throughout the EU. Once the members have been selected for the year, you are invited to join the Orchestra to rehearse and perform major works on international stages all over the world. There are two rounds of auditions in the UK and Ireland: Preliminaries are held in Birmingham, Cork, Dublin, Glasgow, London and Manchester; Finals are held in London and Dublin.

www.euyo.org.uk

National Association of Youth Theatres   14 to adult

The Association supports the development of youth theatre activity through training, advocacy, participation programmes and information services. Its Big Youth Theatre Festival is an outdoor event including opportunities to perform, take part in a wide range of workshops, see others perform and meet youth theatre members from other countries.

www.nayt.org.uk

National Student Drama Festival, Sheffield   16+

The 2012 Festival will take place in Sheffield on 22nd to 30th June in association with Sheffield Theatres, University of Sheffield, Sheffield Hallam University and partnered by the Royal Shakespeare Company, London International Festival of Theatre, Old Vic Tunnels, Stephen Joseph Theatre and the Menier Chocolate Factory amongst others.   The Festival is going international with a nine-day celebration of young people's theatre and will feature the best of British work alongside exceptional productions by young people from across the world. It is for anyone who wants to get involved with drama and the creative industries and is a place where the most inspirational work from diverse, young and emerging artists is celebrated and presented alongside workshops from leading professionals from around the world.

www.nsdf.org.uk

National Youth Orchestra   13-19

One of the world's finest youth orchestras, the National Youth Orchestra (NYO) draws together each year over 150 talented musicians, aged up to 19, from all over the UK. The orchestra meets during the school holidays at New Year, Easter and Summer for intensive two-week periods of coaching and rehearsal with NYO Professors - leading professional musicians and teachers - and some of the world's finest conductors and soloists.

www.nyo.org.uk

National Youth Orchestras of Scotland   **12-21**

The National Youth Orchestras of Scotland (NYOS) provides top-class music education and performance experience for young musicians (ages 12 to 21) throughout Scotland. Running six national youth ensembles, NYOS organises training, intensive rehearsals and national and international concert tours. As well as running the six orchestras, NYOS is committed to introducing musical experiences to all of Scotland's young people.

www.nyos.co.uk

Year Out Drama   **18+**

This is a full-time programme providing an intensive practical drama course with a theatre company feel. The course includes Acting, Directing, Design, Costume, Voice Work, Movement, Text Study, Theatre Trips and at least four full-scale performances during the year, including a production at the Edinburgh Fringe.

www.yearoutdrama.com

Art and Design

Whether marvelling at masterpieces of the Renaissance or producing your own portfolio of design ideas, you can use a gap year to develop new insights into the world of art and design.

Art History Abroad   16/17+

AHA's six-week course involves travelling throughout Italy to study at first hand many masterpieces of Italian art. The programme includes visits to Venice (10 nights), Verona (4 nights), Florence (10 nights), Siena (4 nights), Naples (4 nights) and Rome (10 nights), together with day excursions to at least six of: Padua, Vicenza, Ravenna, Modena, Urbino, Pisa, San Gimignano, Arezzo, Orvieto, Pompeii and Tivoli.

www.arthistoryabroad.com

KLC School of Design, London   18+

The one-week Introduction to Interior Decoration at the KLC Studio in Chelsea gives an insight into the whole process of interior design. The approach is practical with a combination of lectures and workshops that demonstrate how to plan a room layout and how to create a cohesive interior style by developing ideas from a basic concept. Also popular is the one-week Introduction to Garden Design.

www.klc.co.uk

Some of the courses listed here could help you decide whether you would like to train for a career as a professional cook; others can lead to gap year employment as a chalet cook; others are specifically geared to help future university students prepare simple meals for survival on something more than beans on toast after leaving home.

Ballymaloe Cookery School, Ireland   16+

Run by Ireland's most famous TV cook Darina Allen, Ballymaloe offers a highly regarded 12-week certificate course, graduates of which are in demand all over the world. There is also a wide range of shorter courses - some suitable for complete beginners, others aimed at more experienced cooks. A special time every day is lunch, when teachers and students sit down together to enjoy a three-course meal, which the students have prepared using recipes from the demonstrations.

www.cookingisfun.ie

Cookie Crumbles, London 15+

Although Cookie Crumbles specialises in fun cookery for younger children, there are occasional workshops for school and college leavers, giving a firm grasp of how to eat well when cooking for yourself in a hall of residence or in a student house.

www.cookiecrumbles.co.uk

Edinburgh School of Food and Wine 16+

Among a wide range of courses, you may be particularly interested in the Edinburgh School's four-week intensive certificate course, designed to help you earn your keep during a gap year. This practical course will give you the fundamental skills needed to cook for, say, a ski chalet or a highland lodge and a grounding in cookery for life. Also highly relevant is the one-week 'survival course', designed to develop your culinary talents through a combination of demonstration and practical sessions.

www.esfw.com

Le Cordon Bleu 18+

You might try the four-week 'Essentials Course' at this world-renowned institute's London School, or you could consider a short course at one of its centres in France, Canada, Japan, Australia, Mexico or South Korea.

www.cordonbleu.edu

Leith's School of Food and Wine, London 17+

The School offers a varied menu of courses for professional cooks and enthusiastic amateurs. Especially relevant for readers of this book is the one-week 'Survival Cooking' course. This is aimed at those leaving home or cooking on their own for the first time and wishing to equip themselves with basic skills and recipes to allow them to cook nutritionally balanced food on a budget. The course also looks at how to make very simple dishes look impressive, and at how humble ingredients can make delicious meals.

www.leiths.com

Nick Nairn Cook School, Scotland   16+

TV chef Nick Nairn is the man behind the Nick Nairn Cook School, a foodie haven built around a single objective: teaching kitchen confidence. The cook school offers a variety of courses, mostly one day, where visitors can pick up new skills, inspiration and knowledge all whilst preparing their own gourmet lunch. The school is hidden away in the foothills of the Trossachs, right at the heart of some of Scotland's finest scenery, yet less than an hour away from Edinburgh or Glasgow.

www.nicknairncookschool.com

The Orchards School of Cookery, Worcestershire   16+

The one- and two-week 'Chalet Cook' courses can show you how to master the art of being a great chalet cook, enabling you to get the most out of a gap year job in the mountains. Alternatively, the five-day 'Off to University' course covers healthy, delicious and affordable meals for students, including easy entertaining.

www.orchardscookery.co.uk

Padstow Seafood School, Cornwall   8-16

TV chef Rick Stein's famous cooking school mostly caters for adults, but does offer half-day courses for students during the Easter and summer holidays.

www.rickstein.com

Tante Marie School of Cookery, Surrey   16+

Renowned for its professional Diploma courses, Tante Marie offers three shorter courses particularly suited to readers of this book. Whether you are keen to go for a gap year job in a stunning location, would like to take your culinary skills to a higher level or just want a short introduction to cooking well for yourself, family and friends, there could be a suitable course for you. The 11-week 'Cordon Bleu Certificate' is highly valued by ski companies and other gap year employers, although you might also consider the four-week 'Essential Skills' course. If you simply want to eat well at university, look at the one- or two-week 'Beginners' courses, offering an introduction to good food and healthy eating.

www.tantemarie.co.uk

Fundraising

We mention at several points in this publication that it will cost you a fairly considerable sum - often several thousand pounds - to participate in some of the projects listed. This is particularly true of many of the international community, environmental or scientific projects.

For example, to go overseas with Project Trust in 2012, you will be expected to raise £5,000, including a deposit of £250. Project Trust will raise another £500 approximately on your behalf to subsidise the full costs of your year abroad.

Organisations such as Project Trust receive no government assistance and all funds must be raised either by project managers or by volunteers like you.

Given that the aim of this book is to provide you with ideas to help develop your personal, learning and thinking skills, we believe that raising sponsorship can be an important part of this process. It shows others your determination and initiative, and it will help you establish in your own mind just how well you can respond to a challenge. You will have to start by learning how to fundraise and how to make the most of the support available.

Experienced organisers of such projects say that most volunteers are surprised by the response to their efforts and many not only hit their target but actually raise more than the sum required. Only a small number each year have problems and even they can usually be helped to find suitable sponsors.

Should you decide to opt for a project with a sizeable participation fee, you will find that the organisers will normally send you, once accepted, a comprehensive pack containing fundraising ideas and information. In addition, there should be an experienced member of staff able to give you help and advice by email or over the telephone.

The list below should give you a clear idea of the level of fundraising support you should look for when researching a possible project:

- **Advice on fundraising:** Does the selection process introduce the idea of fundraising through a seminar or workshop, encouraging you to think about it constructively?

- **Ongoing support:** What mechanism exists for you to keep the organisers informed of your progress? If you are struggling, do they provide practical advice?

- **Fundraising meetings:** Will you be invited to one or more fundraising meetings, where you can get together with fellow volunteers to share ideas and experiences?

- **Bulletin board:** Is there a website bulletin board allowing you and your fellow volunteers to keep in touch?

Fundraising ideas

The best starting point is always to look inside yourself! There should be no need to turn your life around completely to raise the required funds. Consider what you are already good at and love doing, then think about how you can use your skills to make the money you will need.

If you are good at music, for example, you could try your hand at busking, performing at various events or offering home tuition.

If your interests are more sporting, you could arrange a tournament where teams pay to enter and you provide the service of organising it and setting up suitable prizes.

If you can cook, you could offer a catering service for dinner parties and other social gatherings.

If you are green-fingered, you could offer a gardening service or bring on seeds and cuttings to sell at every opportunity.

If none of these applies, you could simply get a part-time job of any sort and start saving regularly to establish your fund.

Once you have a service to offer, goods to sell or a job to find, turn first to your immediate circle of family, friends and school, college or other social contacts, perhaps in a youth or sports club. If they can't offer you direct support, ask them to think about who they could put you in touch with, or who they might be prepared to approach on your behalf. Before long, you should have a long list of potential customers/employers/sponsors!

While you are raising money, don't forget that you will have other things to buy. You might, for example, need a top quality sleeping bag or rucksack, both of which are likely to be expensive. Baggage insurance is another important extra.

When you go, you will need to take some spending money with you: perhaps around £1,000 for a year-long project, although this can depend upon which country you go to. Even if you can afford it, you shouldn't think of taking so much money overseas that you might be tempted to live and travel in a way that would not sit easily with your role as a volunteer.

Managing Risk

Many of the suggestions in this book contain an element of risk. That is part of their attraction…and you will no doubt see little point in trekking through a jungle or across a mountain range if you are going to be as cosy and safe all the time as you are in an armchair at home. Nevertheless, we could not possibly encourage you to take unnecessary risks and we recommend that you venture overseas only with a reputable organisation with experienced leaders and stringent operating procedures designed to avoid foolhardy misadventure.

We cover a broad range of health and safety issues in our brief quiz on page 61 and we would ask you to spend some time

reading this section and visiting the recommended websites. Amongst them, the *Know before you go* site managed by the Foreign and Commonwealth Office is absolutely essential.

In addition, we suggest that you use the checklist below when choosing an organisation with which to undertake your trip. This will help to ensure that you are in safe hands and will be travelling responsibly.

- **Crisis Management:** Is there a comprehensive crisis management policy in place? How robust is it and how are staff trained to implement it?

- **UK Support:** Does the organisation maintain a 24-hour emergency telephone line for family and friends in the UK?

- **Insurance:** Does the organisation have a comprehensive company insurance policy with a specialist provider?

- **Leaders:** What is the organisation's recruitment policy in relation to the experience and qualifications of expedition leaders? What knowledge do they have of the countries they work in? Do they have relevant language and first aid skills? Does the Criminal Records Bureau carry out checks of their backgrounds?

- **Risk Assessment:** Do expedition leaders undertake daily monitoring of activities in order to maintain the safety of participants? Are written risk assessments available for consultation? Are participants encouraged to carry out their own risk assessments during an expedition?

- **In-Country Support:** Do leaders have up-to-date contact lists for medical and logistical support in the country you will be visiting?

- **Participant Preparation:** What level of pre-departure training and/or in-country orientation is provided for participants?

- **Equipment:** How often is equipment reviewed and replaced? Is safety equipment provided as standard? Do leaders carry comprehensive first aid kits?

- **Transport:** How do leaders assess in-country transport? Is there a policy regarding the use of public or private transport options? Is road transport undertaken at night?

- **Responsible Travel:** What is the organisation's policy in relation to monitoring and minimising the long-term impact of expeditions such as the one you are considering? Is there a long-term commitment to cultural sensitivity and sustainable development?

- **Financial Transparency:** Can the organisation demonstrate that your financial contributions are spent directly on the project and nowhere else?

- **Feedback:** Is there evidence that feedback from participants and staff is assessed and acted upon where necessary to improve future provision?

A final word. While we have tried our best, as publishers of this book, to ensure that you understand the nature of potential hazards overseas - how to recognise and overcome them - we must stress that you cannot rely totally on us or even on the very best provider of specialist gap year activities. You must use your own common sense and initiative to help you to spend your time as safely as possible.

Finding a Focus

When you have researched the ideas in this book, photocopy these pages and complete a worksheet for each project, trip or expedition that interests you. Our 10-point plan will help you focus on finding the right programme to develop your personal learning and thinking skills.

Name of organisation
Type of activity
1. What is it that appeals to me? *(Gaining relevant experience, travel, helping others, earning money)*
2. Am I eligible? *(Right age, available at the right time, suitable qualifications)*
3. What exactly will I be doing? *(Working with others, undertaking/learning about research methods, food)*
4. How will I benefit from this programme?
5. How will other people benefit from my involvement?

6. How much will it cost? *(Total Budget, raising funds, putting down a deposit)*

7. Who will I be signing up with? *(Commercial company, registered charity)*

8. What do I need to arrange? *(Travel, insurance, health check, vaccinations)*

9. Is there any pre-programme training or briefing?

10. What happens afterwards? *(Debriefing, maintain contact with organisations/ providers, inform future participants, obtain certificate recording my achievements)*

Am I Ready for a Trip Abroad?

If you are planning to travel abroad as part of your personal development, try our brief quiz to see how well prepared you are!

1. **INSURANCE ISSUES**
   - (a) I will investigate a range of different types of insurance to cover my travel and placement/project □
   - (b) I will take out travel insurance for the journeys to and from my placement/project □
   - (c) I guess that I'm on our family annual travel insurance and that my parents' insurance policies will cover all eventualities □

2. **THE COUNTRY I INTEND TO VISIT**
   - (a) I have researched the laws and customs of my planned destination as well as the usual food, currency and weather type research □
   - (b) I have looked at holiday websites to find out about the country I intend to visit □
   - (c) I'll pick up everything I need to know just by being in the country for several months □

3. **VISAS AND PERMITS**
   - (a) I have checked out the necessary visas and work permits for the country I intend to visit □
   - (b) I will see if I need a visa □
   - (c) Someone will sort out whatever has to happen about a visa for me □

4. **HEALTH**
   - (a) I will check with my local surgery to see if I need any special injections or healthcare for the country I am visiting a couple of months before the departure date □
   - (b) I will ask my mum to take a look on the internet to see if there is anything I need to do about health care arrangements for my visit □
   - (c) I won't bother to do anything special about healthcare as I am young and healthy □

5. **SAFETY**
   - (a) I have seriously considered a number of ways of ensuring my safety when I am on my placement and I have discussed safety plans with my family □
   - (b) I am always careful about my well being and I won't need to do anything extra for my placement □
   - (c) I have no safety worries and I can look after myself □

How did you do?

If you answered (a) to all the questions then you have made a good start. All (b) then you have a bit more work to do. All (c) then you really must do a lot more research.

Points to consider

1. Insurance issues

It'll never happen to me!

It can happen to you; things can go wrong. You could fall ill or have an accident; you could have money or luggage stolen; your visit might be cancelled or cut short through injury or illness; your family may need to fly out to be with you if there is a serious incident. So take out insurance. Make sure it's comprehensive and covers you for medical and repatriation costs as well as any dangerous sports or activities.

If you get injured or ill as a result of drugs or alcohol, your insurance may be invalidated and your travel operator can refuse to fly you home.

2. The country I intend to visit

You must read up on the laws and customs of your chosen destination, to avoid offending people or breaking local laws, however unwittingly. The best starting point for this is the Foreign and Commonwealth Office, with its 'Know before you go' awareness campaign aimed at encouraging British travellers to prepare better before going overseas. Visit the website at: **www.fco.gov.uk/knowbeforeyougo** or telephone 0845 850 2829.

If you are thinking about taking drugs whilst on holiday abroad or bringing some back with you, stop and think - otherwise your trip of a lifetime could end up lasting a lifetime in jail! Bear in mind that: 2,528 British nationals were detained overseas during 2005, a third of them for drugs-related offences; many countries outside the UK refuse to grant bail before trial and may detain people in solitary confinement; you will still get a criminal record in the UK if arrested with drugs abroad; if you've been caught with drugs abroad, you're unlikely ever to be allowed to visit that country again.

3. Passports, Visas and Work Permits

If you wish to travel abroad you must hold a full ten-year passport, even for a day trip. Apply in good time. In the UK, you can get advice from the Identity and Passport Service website at **www.direct.gov.uk/passports** or call them on the Passport Advice Line on 0300 222 0000 (open 8am to 8pm Mon-Fri and 9am to 5pm weekends & public holidays). Some countries have an immigration requirement for a passport to remain valid for a minimum period (usually at least six months) beyond the date of entry to the country. Therefore, if appropriate, ensure your passport is in good condition and valid for at least six months at the date of your return. This is a requirement of the country concerned, not the UK Passport Service, and any questions should be addressed to their Consulate or Embassy.

Outside the UK, you should get advice in an emergency from the nearest British Embassy, High Commission or Consulate. Staff can issue standard replacement passports in most places, and all missions are able to issue emergency passports if more appropriate.

If you plan to travel outside British territories, you may require a visa to enter the country you are going to. Check visa requirements with your project organiser or travel agent or contact the Consulate or Embassy of the country you plan to visit.

If you plan to work outside the European Union, you will need to obtain a valid work permit before you go.

Some Passport Tips:

- Make a note of your passport number, date and place of issue (or take a photocopy), and keep separately in a safe place.
- Check your passport expiry date.
- Write the full details of your next of kin in your passport.
- Leave a photocopy with a friend or relative at home.
- Take a second means of photo-identification with you.
- Keep your passport in the hotel safe and carry a photocopy with you.
- If your passport is lost or stolen overseas, contact the nearest British Embassy, High Commission or Consulate immediately for advice.

4. Health

- Check the Department of Health website at: **www.nhs.uk/Healthcareabroad** for general medical advice for travellers.

- Check what vaccinations you need with your GP at least six weeks before you travel.

- Check if your medication is legal in the country that you are visiting.

- Pack all medication in your hand luggage.

- If you are taking prescribed medication, take the prescription and a doctor's letter with you.

- If you are travelling within the European Economic Area or Switzerland, you should get a free European Health Insurance Card (EHIC) by visiting the Department of Health website as above. You can also obtain the EHIC by completing the Department of Health leaflet 'Health Advice for Travellers' (HAFT), available through most UK Post Offices or by telephoning 0845 606 2030. The EHIC entitles you to free or reduced-cost medical care but you will still need medical and travel insurance.

- Be safe in the sun. Avoid excessive sunbathing, especially between 11am and 3pm, and wear a high factor sunscreen.

- Drink plenty of water. If you drink alcohol or use some kinds of drugs your body can become dehydrated, especially in a hot climate.

- Find out the local emergency number and the address of the nearest hospital when you arrive overseas. Your rep, local guide or project manager should know.

5. Safety

Be aware of what is going on around you and keep away from situations that make you feel uncomfortable. Avoid potentially dangerous 'no-go' areas, in particular after dark. Use your common sense and make sure you are constantly assessing and reassessing your personal safety. Be aware of drugs - these have been used in incidents of rape, so keep your wits about you.

Keep an eye on your possessions. Never leave your luggage unattended or with someone you don't completely trust. Be aware of pickpockets, who tend to operate in crowded areas, and lock up your luggage with padlocks. Make sure you have copies of all important documents such as your passport, tickets, insurance policy, itinerary and contact details. Keep these separate from the originals and leave copies with your family and friends.

Work out how much money you'll need on a daily basis and work to a realistic budget. Be sure to take enough money, as the Foreign and Commonwealth Office can't send you home free of charge If you run out!

Finally, tell friends and family your plans before you go and keep in regular contact, especially if you change your plans. Consider taking a roam-enabled mobile and use text or email to keep in contact. Don't promise too much - promising to call home every day is unrealistic and will only cause your family and friends to worry when you don't!

Further Information

Best Gap Year

This site will provide you with worldwide gap year jobs, courses and travel opportunities. From Winter jobs in a ski resort or summer sports teaching courses is in Australia to medical projects in China. It offers a huge range of ideas across the world with opportunities to take part in conservation and community projects, teaching, and sports and volunteering. It also provides valuable advice on gap year planning, health and other issues. Visit the website: **www.bestgapyear.co.uk**

Foreign & Commonwealth Office Website

The Foreign and Commonwealth Office website offers lots of advice for anyone thinking of embarking on gap year travel from top tips on insurance and money to advice on staying healthy and getting the right visa, you will find all you need to know to plan the safest and most enjoyable gap year travel.

www.fco.gov.uk/en/travel-and-living-abroad/gapyear

InterHealth

InterHealth specialises in providing detailed and specific travel health advice tailored to remote and exotic destinations. Its website includes a section for gap year travellers. The online shop can supply everything from first aid kits to mosquito nets and water purification tablets. **www.interhealth.org.uk**

Gapyear.com

Gapyear.com is a social media and travel advice website devoted to giving you everything you could possibly need when planning or taking a gap year. It hosts and supports a community that is passionate about real travel and ready to share experience and advice. The community is backed up with expert guides.

Gapyear.com was created by backpackers, for backpackers and covers everything you need to know for your adventure, including gap year jobs, gap year travel packages and gap year volunteering.

www.gapyear.com

Gap Advice

Gapadvice.org was founded in June 2005 to provide an independent source of impartial advice and information for people of all ages looking to take a gap week, month or year. It provides advice for young people after leaving school, for undergraduates and those who have just graduated as well as those looking for career breaks. It contains information on considering your gap year, investigating it, organising it, doing it etc., all covered in a comprehensive five step plan.

www.gapadvice.org

Hostelling International

Youth hostels can provide you with reliable, reasonably priced accommodation in many parts of the world. Hostelling International is the brand name of more than 90 Youth Hostel Associations in 90 countries, operating 4,000 plus hostels. Unlike bland motels, impersonal hotels or dodgy backpacker rooms, youth hostels are usually fun, lively meeting places, full of like-minded people. Visit the website at: **www.hihostels.com**

Objective Team

Your school or college may be willing to organise a safety and security awareness training course to help you prepare for a gap year. One organisation specialising in this type of work is Objective Team. Visit their website at:
www.objectivegapyear.com

STA Travel

Specialists in cheap flights, adventure trips and travel deals for young people, STA Travel have several pages of gap year travel tips on their website at: **www.statravel.co.uk**

Suggested Reading List

Before You Go: The Ultimate Guide to Planning your Gap Year
- Tom Griffiths, Bloomsbury, 2003

The Gap Year Book: The Definitive Guide to Planning and Taking a Year Out (Lonely Planet Gap Year Guide)
- Joseph Bindloss and Charlotte Hindle, Lonely Planet Publications, 2005

The Gap-year Guidebook 2011: Everything You Need to Know About Taking a Gap-year or Year Out
- Alex Sharratt, John Catt Educational Ltd, 2010

Taking a Gap Year: The Essential Guide to Taking a Year Out
- Susan Griffith, Vacation Work Publications, 2005

Don't Tell Mum: Hair-raising Messages Home from Gap-year Travellers
- Simon Hoggart and Emily Monk, Atlantic Books, 2007

The Gap Year Handbook: An Essential Guide to Adventure Travel
- Tim Beacon, Authorsonline, 2005

Gap Year Volunteer: A Guide to Making It a Year to Remember
- Summersdale Publishers, 2006

The Backpacker's Bible: Your Essential Guide to Round-the-World Travel
- Suzanne King and Elaine Robertson, Portico, 2010

The Travellers Good Health Guide
- Dr Ted Lankester, Sheldon Press, 2006

Worldwide Volunteering
- Worldwide Volunteer Organisation, How To Books, 2004

Green Volunteers 8th Edition: The World Guide to Voluntary Work in Nature Conservation
- Fabio Ausenda, Green Volunteers, 2011

World Volunteers: The World Guide to Humanitarian and Development Volunteering
- Fabio Ausenda and Erin McCloskey, Crimson Publishing, 2008

Archaeo-Volunteers: The World Guide to Archaeological and Heritage Volunteering
- Fabio Ausenda and Erin McCloskey, Green Volunteers, 2009

The Rough Guide to First-Time Around the World
- Doug Lansky, Rough Guides, 2010

Improve Your Grades! - Revision Courses

The following independent colleges offer specific retake and intensive revision courses, giving you the opportunity to improve your performance in a wide range of subjects during the Easter vacation.

Abbey Colleges

The Abbey Colleges are part of the Alpha Plus Group - formerly Davies, Laing and Dick Education Group - which currently comprises twenty independent schools, colleges and sixth form colleges, Lyn Fry Associates and the Best Practice Network. Abbey Colleges in Birmingham, Cambridge, London and Manchester offer intensive retake courses for GCSE and AS and A Level.

www.abbeycolleges.co.uk

Ashbourne Independent Sixth Form College, Kensington, London

Easter revision courses seek to motivate students to strive for the highest grades at A level and GCSE, and to develop independence and self-reliance. As a private college, Ashbourne is able to offer classes which average five students per group.

www.ashbournecollege.co.uk

Bosworth Independent College, Northampton

Relatively new in terms of tradition, Bosworth Independent College boasts an ever growing reputation for academic excellence, providing Easter revision in addition to GCSE, A level, University Foundation Programmes and English Language courses

www.bosworthcollege.com

Cambridge Centre for Sixth-Form Studies

Easter Revision courses can make a major difference to your examination prospects. Classes are very small and teachers are experienced not just in covering the common core in each subject, but also the requirements for each specification.

www.ccss.co.uk

Collingham College, Kensington, London

Intensive tuition in small classes enables individual needs to be met. Groups are Board-specific as appropriate and are formed according to syllabus, topics, texts and so on. The courses are planned to give a clear understanding of the essentials of the syllabus and to teach exam techniques, so that you can use your knowledge to best effect.

www.collingham.co.uk

Duff Miller Sixth Form College, South Kensington, London

Duff Miller offers Easter Revision courses across a wide range of A Level and GCSE subjects. They act to inspire, motivate and fulfil academic potential. The primary emphasis of the revision courses is to enhance subject knowledge and establish a rigorous, disciplined and effective approach, resulting in peak exam performance.

www.duffmiller.com

Harrogate Tutorial College

Easter Revision courses at Harrogate are designed to help students achieve examination grades well above those they originally expected, but are not intended for students who have done little or no work in their subjects. The small classes - average four, maximum eight students - generate an informal, student-centred approach with the emphasis on high quality work.

www.htcuk.org

Justin Craig Education

Justin Craig Education offer revision courses in all the main AS /A2 and GCSE subjects at a choice of 10 residential or day centres around the country. Teachers ensure that all students are given the necessary assistance and motivation to revise quickly and productively.

www.justincraig.ac.uk

Lansdowne College, London

Lansdowne College has run Easter Revision courses for over 20 years, helping thousands of students to realise their full academic potential at both GCSE and A Level, and enabling them to progress onto their chosen path for their studies. Students often find themselves unaware of exactly what the examiners are looking for and subsequently unsure of what makes an A grade answer. The Easter Revision courses remedy this by focusing not just on the subject content, but also on extensive and comprehensive examination preparation, including a free mock examination at the end of the course.

www.lansdownecollege.com

Mander Portman Woodward (MPW)

MPW is an independent sixth-form college group, with colleges in London, Birmingham and Cambridge. In addition to full-time GCSE courses, AS courses and A2 courses over a very wide range of subjects and with no restrictions on subject combinations, MPW offers intensive A level and GCSE retake courses and revision courses over Easter. Characterising all courses is an absolute maximum of eight students within any one class and a strong emphasis on exam technique and exam practice.

www.mpw.co.uk

Millfield School, Somerset

On its Easter Revision course, Millfield offers specialist tuition at GCSE, AS and A2 level, in a broad range of subjects to small groups of students, providing a balance of taught content and rehearsal of technique. Students from all schools are welcome. Courses are offered on both a residential and non-residential basis.

www.millfieldenterprises.com

Oxford Tutorial College

Oxford Tutorial College organises short intensive revision courses at Easter and supplementary teaching to support the work being done at school. There is a mixture of individual tuition and small group seminars.

www.otc.ac.uk

Rochester Independent College, Kent

Intensive Easter revision courses at Rochester provide an opportunity to gain an overview of the syllabus and a chance to practise applying knowledge to real examination questions. This helps with recall of facts and hones skills required for accurate question interpretation and structuring full and concise answers. Most importantly, the courses give a real confidence boost at a crucial time.

www.rochester-college.org

Taster Courses, Summer Schools and Open Days

Almost all universities and colleges organise pre-application Open Days, giving you an opportunity to visit the campus, meet some of the staff and students, and attend a short talk on a subject in which you are interested. Details of these days can be found in the *Open Days* booklet published by UCAS.

We focus here on courses that some universities and colleges provide to give you a more detailed opportunity to experience academic and social life on campus. Please note that we refer to *Taster Courses* for the sake of clarity but universities are independent institutions and don't always use the same terminology. It is, therefore, not unusual to find *Taster Courses* described as Summer Schools or Academies (at any time of year!), Campus Days or Find Out More Days.

Duration

Course lengths vary: some are one-day courses only, others may last a weekend or even a week. Most courses are free. You may have the chance to stay overnight on campus.

Format

Most *Taster Courses* include lectures, discussions and tutorial sessions, so that you can meet the departmental staff and get hands-on experience using the facilities. This can provide an important insight into how the university or college operates. *Taster Courses* should also allow you to find out about other aspects of undergraduate life, such as sporting, musical, drama and cultural activities, accommodation and other amenities.

Benefits of Attending a Taster Course

- You are more likely to choose a higher education course to suit your interests and abilities and to avoid an unsuitable one.
- You can highlight your attendance in the personal statement section of your UCAS application.
- You may find that a course or campus is not for you, and decide to reject it in favour of others.
- You can discuss your impressions with admissions tutors at universities or colleges during interviews.

Science and Technology tasters

In addition to the Taster Courses listed on the following pages, see pages 33 to 36 for details of the science and technology tasters organised by Headstart and the Smallpeice Trust.

University of Aberdeen Summer School for Access

The Summer School is a ten-week, full-time programme of study, which runs from June to August each year. You have to undertake four courses and complete coursework and exams, on successful completion of which (at minimum Grade 12 out of 20) you will be guaranteed a place on an undergraduate programme at the University of Aberdeen. You may also use the Summer School for entry into other universities across the UK, although you must contact the other institutions and agree their entry requirements before you start.

If you are a student from within the European Union, you are not normally required to pay tuition fees for the Summer School and free accommodation may also be available, based on household income and expenditure. For full details see the website: **www.abdn.ac.uk/lifelonglearning/ssa** or email: **SSA-Aberdeen@abdn.ac.uk**

Aberystwyth University

The Recruitment & Marketing Office can arrange on-campus taster days and workshops for school and college groups. Please email **marketing@aber.ac.uk** if you would like to discuss the day/residential programmes available at the University.

Aston University, Birmingham

Aston organises a programme of events aimed at providing a taster of university life in specific subject areas, including: Biology, Business, Chemistry, English Language, Law, Mathematics, Modern Foreign Languages (French, German, Spanish and Chinese), Optometry, Pharmacy, Psychology, Politics and Sociology.

For further information, please contact: **morrisa@aston.ac.uk** Telephone: 0121 204 4787 Website: **www.aston.ac.uk/study/undergraduate/schliaison**

University of Birmingham School of Engineering

There may be some opportunities to experience engineering by attending one-day taster courses in the five Schools of Engineering during the spring/summer. For full details visit the website at **www.birmingham.ac.uk**. Headstart and Focus run engineering and science courses at Birmingham - visit the website: **www.headstartcourses.org.uk**

University College, Birmingham

University College offers a Summer School in various subjects. Full time - 3 days/2 nights. Limited spaces only. Also Master Classes offered in nine various subjects on one morning or afternoon. Limited spaces only.

For further details on summer school and master classes, please contact Ruth Walton, telephone 0121 243 0042 or email: **ruthwalton@ucb.ac.uk** or visit the website: **www.ucb.ac.uk**

Bradford College

The college offers a variety of taster days for courses in both further and higher education. To attend or request more information about their taster days, contact the Education Liaison Team Leader, telephone 01274 433084 or email: **educationliaison@bradfordcollege.ac.uk**

University of Chichester

Several departments at the University of Chichester run taster days, in which you can sample lectures or participate in workshops. In some cases, these events are open to all prospective applicants, while others invite people who have already applied, to help them make their final choice. You can book online for taster days - usually held in March/April - in the following areas: Business and IT Management, Humanities, Arts, Sport Science and Sports Studies, Education and Teaching and Social Sciences.

Further information can be found at:
www.chiuni.ac.uk/tasterdays

Cornwall College, Newquay

Offers university course taster days on various dates between October and June. These taster days give prospective students the opportunity to look around the campus and its facilities, talk to programme lecturers and discover more about the course of interest. Students can also find out about tuition fees and the financial support available, meet current students and discover more about student life in Cornwall. Booking is essential. For further details, please telephone 01637 857 957 or visit the website at: **www.cornwall.ac.uk**

University of Exeter, Cornwall Campus Open Days

A University of Exeter, Cornwall Campus Open Day is packed with opportunities for you to find out if the University of Exeter is right for you. As a visitor to the small and friendly campus, near Falmouth, you can spend a day attending sample lectures, discussing programme options with the leading academics and finding out from current students what it's really like to study at a top research-led university in a stunning location. There are also tours of the campus and facilities, including the on-site accommodation, student bar and sports centre. Prospective Geology and Mining Engineering students can visit our test mine. At the Cornwall Campus programmes are offered in Biosciences, English, Environmental Science, Flexible Combined Honours, Geography, Geology, History, Mining Engineering, Politics and Renewable Energy.

For full details, please visit the website at: **www.exeter.ac.uk/visit**

University of Exeter, College of Engineering, Mathematics and Physical Sciences

The Pre-University Physics Course is offered in July. For further details please contact **emps@exeter.ac.uk** or visit the website at: **www.exeter.ac.uk/pupc**

Glyndwr University

Glyndwr University hosts a number of open days and interactive sessions each year which could help you if you have not yet made the decision to enter HE. The focus is on demystifying HE, increasing awareness of the opportunities available, answering questions about finance and support, building confidence and skills, and getting to know the campus and facilities.

For further details, contact the Widening Access Team at: **sid@glyndwr.ac.uk** or visit the website at: **www.glyndwr.ac.uk**

University of Leeds

Leeds has an international reputation for its teaching and research. It offers a range of courses and opportunities to help you develop into an articulate, highly-skilled and confident graduate ready to pursue the career of your choice.

Find out more about Leeds and what it offers at the website, **www.leeds.ac.uk**, and visit one of the open days. If you make Leeds one of your five choices you may be invited for a detailed departmental visit.

Register for open days at:
www.leeds.ac.uk/opendays

London Taster Course Programme

With over 160 courses in 70 different subject areas at numerous university institutions, the Taster Course Programme provides the opportunity to experience life as a university student in the subject area of your choice, ranging from medicine and dentistry to drama and film studies. The taster courses run from half a day to one week, and are usually available between March and July. All courses are non-residential and provided free of charge. You may apply for up to three courses via the online application form. The Careers Group, University of London administers the programme and in 2011 the following colleges participated. (please visit the website at: **www.london.ac.uk/tasters** or email: **tastercourses@london.ac.uk** for an up-to-date list of participating colleges in 2012):

Birkbeck:
Law
Psychology
History of Art

Central School of Speech and Drama:
Voice
Choices in Drama

City University, London:
Journalism
Radiography
Speech & Language Therapy
Midwifery
Nursing
Optometry
Aeronautical Engineering
Automotive & Mechanical Engineering
Civil Engineering
Electrical & Electronic / Computer Systems / Multi-Media/
        Bio-Medical Engineering
Computing
Law
Economics
Politics
Psychology
Sociology
Event Management
Music

Goldsmiths:
Politics
Media & Communications

Heythrop College:
Psychology and Philosophy
Abrahamic Faiths and International Conflict
Philosophy
Theology
Philosophy, Religion & Ethics
Psychology and Theology

Imperial College:
How Maths Drives Computing
Future Computing

King's College:
Nursing
French Studies
German Studies
Midwifery
Nutrition
Theology & Religious Studies

London Metropolitan:
Law
Governance & Internal Relations
Business

London School of Economics & Political Science (LSE):
Anthropology
Geography and Environment
International History
Sociology

London South Bank University:
Business, Computing, Marketing, Management and Accounting
Product Design
Nursing
Allied Health Professions

Queen Mary:
Mathematics
Business & Management
Economics & Finance
Global Change: Environment, Economy and Development
History
Law
Dentistry
Chemistry
Molecules of Life
Electronic Engineering
Computing
Design & Innovation
Options for Women in Engineering
Aerospace Engineering
Dental Materials
Materials Science
Mechanical Engineering
Medical Engineering
Medical Materials

Queen Mary continued:
Sustainable Energy Engineering
Technical Alternatives to Medicine and Dentistry
Physics
Astrophysics

The Careers Group, University of London:
Careers in Medicine
Career Options for Science, Technology, Engineering and
Mathematics
Careers in Law

Royal Holloway:
Aspects of the Classical World
Philosophy
Exploring Languages
History
Bioscience
Computer Science
Global Connections
Mathematics
Physics

Royal Veterinary College:
Veterinary Nursing
Bio-veterinary Sciences
Veterinary Medicine

School of Oriental & African Studies:
Languages and Cultures
Arts and Humanities

St George's Hospital:
A Taste of Medicine

The Courtauld Institute of Art:
Art and Its Histories

UCL:
Discovering the Ancient World
Bio-Diversity in Urban Spaces
An understanding of the construction industry
Introduction to Chemical Engineering
Women in Engineering
Engineering and Quality of Life

UCL continued:
> Threatening the Weimar Republic (1918-1933)
> Electronic and Electrical Engineering
> Workshop on French cinema
> Women in Mathematics
> An Introduction to Medical Physics
> East European language tasters: Finnish, Hungarian, Romanian, Serbian/Croatian, Ukrainian

University of East London:
> Psychology

University of Greenwich:
> Film and TV Production
> Computing
> English Language, Language Teaching and Literature
> Mathematics

University of London Institute in Paris:
> Cinéma français: Culture et Langue

University of Westminster:
> Biology

Loughborough University

Engineering Experience - Loughborough's Schools of Engineering have been running this highly successful two-day event for the last 23 years. Engineering Experience takes place once a year - 2012 dates are 27th & 28th March. Open to year 12 (lower sixth form) students, the event, which costs £45 to take part in (to cover meals and accommodation), gives an insight into engineering at university. During their stay at the University, students have the opportunity to visit six different engineering departments (Aeronautical and Automotive Engineering, Mechanical and Manufacturing Engineering, Civil and Building Engineering, Electronic and Electrical Engineering, Chemical Engineering and Materials), learn about different engineering options, talk to lecturers and tutors about engineering courses and experience student accommodation, the Students' Union and catering. Spaces are limited.

For further information visit the website at: **www.engexp.info**

Newcastle College

Taster courses are offered in Art and Design, Beauty and Complementary Therapies, Business Management and Computing. Construction and Civil Engineering, Engineering and Science, Health Care and Public Services, Music, Media and Performing Arts, Sport and Exercise, Travel, Aviation and Hospitality. Taster courses are usually run in conjunction with open days which take place in March, June and October.

For further details, please contact 0191 200 4874, email: **martin.hall@ncl-coll.ac.uk** or visit the website at: **www.newcastlecollege.co.uk/undergraduate**

Newcastle University

Newcastle University holds three Visit Days each year, which are an excellent opportunity to see the University at its bustling best and find out more about the subjects you're interested in. Find out more about the Visit Days and other opportunities to get a feel for student life at Newcastle: **www.ncl.ac.uk/undergraduate/visit**

University of Reading Food and Nutritional Sciences Summer School

Are you a young scientist with an interest in a career in food? The Department of Food and Nutritional Sciences at Reading offers an annual short introductory course in late June/early July for lower 6th form students (Year 12). The course is sponsored by manufacturing and retail companies in the food industry. For further information, contact Nikki Spong **n.spong@reading.ac.uk** or visit the website: **www.reading.ac.uk/food**

Royal Agricultural College (RAC)

The RAC's two-day taster course is aimed mainly at 16 to 19 year olds but it may also be of interest to more mature students. It gives an insight into the career opportunities that exist in the food and land-based industries, both in the UK and worldwide. It also provides an opportunity to learn more about the courses on offer at the College.

For full details and a downloadable application form, visit the website at: **www.rac.ac.uk** or email: **jenny.maguire@rac.ac.uk**

The date for 2012 is 26th to 27th June.

Shrewsbury College of Arts and Technology

Secondary school pupils from around Shropshire are being invited to 'taster sessions' at Shrewsbury College to give them an insight into life in Further Education. Tasters are mainly intended for Year 11 pupils, but can also include those from years 9 and 10. The College has two campuses, at London Road and Radbrook. Tasters at London Road will include Art and Design, Computing and IT, Performing Arts, Public Services, Sports Studies and Travel and Tourism. Also at London Road will be tasters run by the Technology Faculty, including Brickwork, Carpentry and Joinery, Painting and Decorating, Electrical Installation, Plumbing, Engineering and Motor Vehicle.

At Radbrook campus, pupils can sample Business and Accounting, Catering, Childcare, Health and Social Care, and Hair and Beauty.

For further details visit the website at: **www.shrewsbury.ac.uk** or telephone 01743 342333.

Sparsholt College

If you are considering a career in the land-based or animal industries, Sparsholt College offers taster days for year 9, 10 and 11 pupils in a range of career areas. For mature students, a tailored seminar is also available on a Saturday in March. These special programmes all carry a nominal cost, but can be valuable in helping to make course and career choices.

Full details can be obtained by emailing:
enquiries@sparsholt.ac.uk

University of Southampton

The University of Southampton will be hosting open days for prospective students and their parents during the early autumn. The programme of events includes both general and subject-specific presentations and drop-in points as well as tours of academic schools, campuses and halls of residence. Advance booking is highly recommended.

For further information, please visit: **www.southampton.ac.uk/visit**

Sutton Trust Summer School

Sutton Trust Summer Schools offer an opportunity to try University life for over 800 young people every year. The programme consists of lectures, seminars and tutorials but also various social activities. The programme runs at Oxford, Bristol, Cambridge, Nottingham and St Andrews Universities.

The Sutton Trust Summer Schools are open to all students in Year 12 at maintained schools or colleges in the UK. Places are limited. Priority will be given to students:

- whose family background has no history of higher education
- whose parents are in non-professional occupations
- who have achieved at least 5 A/A*'s at GCSE
- Please visit the website for full eligibility criteria

Courses are available in areas including: English, History of Art, Theology, Drama, Languages, History, Philosophy, Sciences, Computer Science, Maths, Social Sciences, Economics, Politics, Law, Engineering, Medicine, Dentistry and Veterinary Science.

The Sutton Trust meets all costs incurred by the student including travel, food and accommodation. For full details, visit the website: **www.suttontrust.com**

Swansea University

Taster courses are available in various subject areas such as engineering, nursing, modern languages and psychology. For further details visit: **www.swansea.ac.uk** or contact the Student Recruitment Office, who may be able to arrange visits, direct via email: **b.m.clark@swansea.ac.uk**

Warwickshire College

Taster days in land-based subjects are offered at Moreton Morrell and Pershore and give an opportunity to experience what it's like to be a student at Warwickshire College. A taster will cover a practical hands-on session and lecture samples in a friendly atmosphere, with knowledgeable and approachable staff and a great countryside location.

For further details of taster days available, visit the website at: **www.warwickshire.ac.uk**

University of the West of Scotland

Summer School is offered at the Dumfries Campus on 2 days per week in business and computing. It gives the opportunity to try out new subjects, experience university life, enhance your qualifications, develop study skills, boost confidence and improve your employability. Contact 01387 702 075 for details.

Introductory level study is also available in other subjects at campuses in Ayr, Dumfries, Hamilton and Paisley, e.g. First Steps to Nursing, First Steps to University, First Steps in IT and Career Planning. These modules are delivered on a part-time basis starting in September, January and June each year. For details contact 0800 027 1000 or visit the website: **www.uws.ac.uk**

Wales Summer University, Aberystwyth - July / August 2012

The Summer University provides a free six-week, full-time, residential (or non-residential) programme for young people from Community First areas in Wales, those receiving ALG or other non-traditional backgrounds. The programme consists of Core Skills together with academic modules (including Art, Business Studies, Biological Sciences, Childhood Studies, Computing and IT, Countryside Management, Creative Writing (in English), English Literature, European Languages, Film and Media Studies, Environmental Studies and Geography, History, International Politics, Law, Mathematics, Physics, Psychology, Sports and Exercise Science - subject to numbers). All students who successfully complete the Summer University will be offered a guaranteed progression route to an appropriate degree scheme at Aberystwyth University, subject to conditions and a reduced offer. For further details contact: **wpsi@aber.ac.uk**

University of York

The University of York will be running a number of taster courses in March 2012, focusing on a range of different subject areas. The aims of these courses are to provide Year 12 students with an insight into university level study, whilst also showing the range of degrees on offer at the University of York. For students who are not sure about what they want to study, or whether university is the right option, taster days are the perfect opportunity to find out more.

For full details of the range of subjects, visit the website at: **www.york.ac.uk**. For further information on taster courses, please contact Sarah Booth at **sarah.booth@york.ac.uk** or tel: 01904 323196.

Subject Index

Note: this index relates primarily to activities mentioned in our brief descriptions of opportunity providers on pages 4 to 68. We cannot guarantee to have covered every activity offered by every provider.

Geographic Index - opportunities overseas

Note: this index relates primarily to countries mentioned in our brief descriptions of opportunity providers on pages 4 to 29. We cannot guarantee to have covered every country offered by every provider.

Index of Taster Course Subjects

*   *Please note that some institutions do not list specific subjects for taster courses. We therefore suggest that you study pages 73 to 87 to see if a campus you would like to visit is included.*

Lookout for the UCAS Open Days and Taster Courses Booklet in January 2012 for further details of available taster courses. Also use the COA taster courses website to select courses which suit your preferred dates and locations. Visit: **www.coa.co.uk/opendays**

Organisation Index

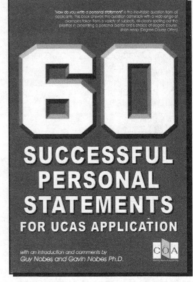